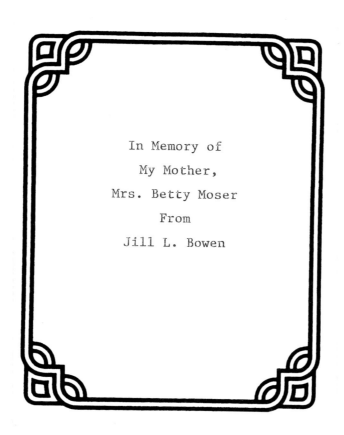

In Memory of
My Mother,
Mrs. Betty Moser
From
Jill L. Bowen

Why Why Why are orangutans so hairy?

First published as hardback in 2006 by
Miles Kelly Publishing Ltd, Bardfield Centre,
Great Bardfield, Essex, CM7 4SLCopyright
© Miles Kelly Publishing Ltd 2006

This 2009 edition published and distributed
by:

Mason Crest Publishers Inc.
370 Reed Road, Broomall, Pennsylvania
19008
(866) MCP-BOOK (toll free)
www.masoncrest.com

Why Why Why—
Are Orangutans So Hairy?
ISBN 978-1-4222-1570-8
Library of Congress Cataloging-in-
Publication data is available

Why Why Why—?
Complete 23 Title Series
ISBN 978-1-4222-1568-5

Printed in the United States of America

Contents

Why are orangutans so hairy?

Fur or hair keeps some animals warm. Animals that have fur or hair are called mammals. Fur also protects from the weather. This hairy orangutan lives in the rainforest. She picks fruit and leaves to eat. She feeds her baby on milk.

The name ORANGUTAN is derived from the Malay language meaning 'old man of the forest.' The actual Malay name is 'Mawas.'

Orangutan

What is a joey?

A joey is a baby kangaroo. When a joey is born it is smaller than your big toe! Even though it is tiny and blind, the joey crawls all the way to its mother's pouch and climbs in. It feeds on milk from its mother.

Joey

Egg-citing news!

Most mammals give birth. This means that they have babies, cubs or kittens. Some strange mammals, such as the duck-billed platypus, lay eggs.

Find out

Were you a beautiful baby, or did you hatch from an egg? Look at old photos of yourself to find out.

Why do some mammals sniff the air?

Many mammals use their noses to get information about the world around them. Their noses are very sensitive to smells. Wild animals, such as deer and rabbits, sniff the air around them to check for signs of danger.

What is the biggest mammal?

The blue whale is—and it's enormous! In fact, it is the biggest animal that has ever lived. Even a baby blue whale is huge—it measures 23 feet in length. All whales are mammals and give birth to their babies, which are called calves.

What a nose!

African elephants have the longest noses! Their noses are called trunks and they can be 8 feet long. Trunks are used for smelling, picking up food, and drinking.

How big is an elephant?

One African elephant can weigh more than 100 people put together. Elephants are the biggest animals that live on land and they can reach 13 feet in height. They spend most of their day eating to keep themselves that huge!

African elephant

Measure

Using a measuring tape, see if you can mark out how long a blue whale calf is.

Blue whale

What is the smallest mammal?

The tiny hog-nosed bat is not much bigger than your thumb! Bats are the only mammals that can fly. They usually sleep during the day and come out at night to look for food.

How do cheetahs run so fast?

Cheetahs have big muscles in their legs and they can run faster than any other animal. These speedy cats run out of breath quickly. This means that the animals they're chasing, such as gazelles, often manage to escape. Cheetahs can reach speeds of over 60 miles an hour!

Cheetah

Why do hares kick?

Hares sometimes kick out at their enemies. Other animals such as foxes try to catch hares to eat them. If the hare sees, smells, or hears an enemy, it can run fast to get away, or kick out with its back legs.

Hare

Run

How fast can you run? Ask an adult to time you next time you are in the park or garden.

Whoosh!

The pronghorn deer is one of the fastest mammals in North America. It runs fast to escape from wolves, which hunt it for food.

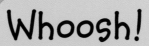

Gazelle

Which mammal is very bouncy?

Kangaroos bounce instead of running. The red kangaroo is a champion jumper and it leaps across the dry deserts of its Australian home. It travels quickly to search for water and food, which are hard to find in a desert.

Are mammals good swimmers?

Some mammals are super swimmers! Whales, dolphins, and seals have bodies that are perfectly shaped for moving through water smoothly and quickly. They have fins and tails instead of arms and legs. Whales and dolphins spend their whole lives in water.

Harp seal

Can seals breathe underwater?

No mammals can breathe underwater—not even seals, whales, and dolphins. Instead, they have to take in all the air they need when they are at the surface of the water, then hold their breath. Some seals can stay underwater for an hour at a time!

Bowhead whale

Diving deep!

The Weddell seal is a daring diver. It plunges down to the deep, dark, cold water of the oceans as it hunts for fish to eat.

What does a killer whale kill?

Killer whales kill squid, fish, seals, and even birds. They are strong swimmers and have sharp, pointed teeth. Killer whales can be friendly. They live in family groups and calves stay with their mothers all their lives!

Swim

You are a mammal and you can learn to swim too! Visit your local pool for some watery fun!

Are polar bears cuddly?

Polar bears may look cuddly with their thick, white fur, but they are fierce hunters. These bears live in the ice-covered lands near the North Pole. Their fur keeps them warm—they even have fur on the soles of their feet so that their toes don't get frost bite!

Polar bear

Lots of lemmings!

A female lemming can have her first babies when she is only 14 days old. From then on, she can have as many as 12 babies every single month!

Why are some animals white?

White animals usually live in places that are covered with snow in winter. A white Arctic hare blends into the snow and hides from enemies. In summer, the snow melts and the hare grows brown fur.

Paint

Paint a snowy scene showing some animals that live in cold places, such as polar bears, seals, and penguins.

How do seals stay warm?

Seals spend a lot of their time underwater in cold parts of the world. They can keep warm because they have thick layers of fat, called blubber, under their skin. Seals also have waterproof fur that stops water getting through to their skin.

Mother seal

Seal pup

Do all mammals sleep at night?

Many mammals sleep during the day and are awake at night. Hyenas often sleep during the hot African day and come out at night to hunt. They catch other animals to eat, or eat food that has been left behind by other hunters, such as lions.

Eye can see it!

Monkey-like tarsiers have huge eyes to help them see in the dark forests where they live. They hunt insects at night using their good eyesight and hearing to help them.

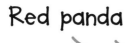

Red panda

Hyena

Why does a red panda come out at night?

Red pandas come out at night to look for their food. They eat mice and lizards as well as birds' eggs and insects. Red pandas live in forests around mountains. During the day they climb trees to snooze and sunbathe!

How do bats find their food?

Bats hunt insects at night when it is dark and difficult to see. They send out special sounds that bounce off an insect and back to the bats' ears. The bats can tell where their food is, and catch it.

Play

Play blind man's bluff. Use a blindfold and discover what it feels like to find your way in the dark.

Why do wolves live in packs?

Wolves live in packs because they hunt together and look after one another. A mother wolf takes good care of her cubs. As the cubs grow, they are brought food from their father and other members of the wolf pack.

Wolves

Cool cats!

Lions may be fierce, but they are also very lazy. They sleep or doze for more than 20 hours a day, keeping cool in the shade!

How many meerkats live together?

Meerkats live in groups of up to 30 animals. A group is called a colony and each colony is made up of several families. While some meerkats search for food, others stand guard and look for enemies, such as hawks.

Meerkats ⟶

What is a group of whales called?

A group of whales is called a pod. Pilot whales live in pods of 20 or more animals that swim and hunt together. Some dolphins live in pods that may have more than 1,000 members.

Count

How many people can you count in your family? Include all your grandparents, aunts, uncles, and cousins.

How big is a baby panda?

Pandas give birth to tiny babies, or cubs. Each cub could fit inside your hand and weighs the same as an apple. Newborn pandas are blind and helpless. They do not open their eyes until they are two or three months old.

Panda

Panda cub

What are baby elephants called?

Baby elephants are called calves. Soon after they are born, elephant calves are able to stand up. Within a few days, they can run around. Elephants live in groups called herds. The adult elephants protect the young from lions and hyenas.

Elephant calf

Big baby!

The baby blue whale is bigger than any other mammal baby. It weighs more than 30 people put together and drinks up to 132 gallons of milk every day.

Measure

How much milk do you drink every day? Use a measuring jug to see how much milk fills up a glass.

Which mammal has the most babies at a time?

The Virginia opossum can have up to 21 babies at a time—more than any other mammal. Each baby opossum is no bigger than a fingertip! If it is attacked, a Virginia opossum lies down and pretends to be dead.

How do tigers catch their food?

Tigers are hunters. Their bodies are perfect for finding, chasing, and killing other animals. Stripy fur helps the tiger blend in with tall grass so they are difficult to spot. When a tiger sees a meal, it runs and pounces. It uses its claws and teeth to kill.

Tiger

Deer

What do bears eat?

Bears eat all kinds of food. Some bears hunt other animals but most eat insects, fruit, and leaves. Sloth bears love to eat termites. They have long claws for digging out termite nests. The bears suck the termites up one at a time!

Sloth bear

Why do dogs hunt in packs?

Wild dogs hunt in packs because they are more likely to get something to eat. By working together they can surround an animal. They may catch a bigger animal than one dog alone could catch.

Work

Working together is best. True or false? Help an adult with the shopping or the housework to find out!

Are rhinos dangerous?

A rhinoceros is one of the most dangerous mammals. Mother rhinos may attack people, or other animals, to protect their babies. They can run fast and they have sharp horns for attacking. Male rhinos also use their horns to fight one another.

Bee-eaters!

Smelly skunks sometimes feed on bees. They roll the bees on the ground to remove the stings before eating them.

Why do some mammals have scales?

Some mammals have scales to protect themselves, rather like a suit of armor. Pangolins are strange ant-eating mammals that live in Africa and Asia. Their bodies are covered in overlapping scales that protect them from other animals— and the stinging bites of ants.

Pangolin

Rhinoceros

What is the stinkiest mammal?

Skunks are very stinky mammals! These stripy creatures shake their tails at an enemy to warn it to stay away. If that doesn't work, the skunk raises its tail and sprays a smelly liquid in its enemy's face!

Make it
Ask an adult to help you make a cardboard suit of armor. How easy is it to move wearing the armor?

Where do jaguars live?

Jaguars live in rain forests in Central and South America. They love water and prefer to stay near rivers, lakes, and swamps. Jaguars hunt deer, turtles, and sloths. They hunt on land or in water—and have even been known to kill crocodiles.

Jaguar

Do sloths spend all day in trees?

Sloths spend nearly all their lives hanging upside down in trees. They only come down to the ground once a week. Sloths are well-known for moving slowly. If they hear other animals nearby they stay still and hope no one notices them.

Sloth

Try it

Measure 16 feet with a measuring tape, then see how slowly you can travel that distance.

Which is the noisiest mammal?

The noisiest mammal of all is the howler monkey. These monkeys howl and whoop at one another across the treetops. Their calls can be heard 3 miles away!

Slowest of all!

The sloth is the slowest animal in the world. In trees it moves along at about 16 feet a minute. On the ground it moves even more slowly—about 6 feet a minute!

Do mammals eat all day?

Some mammals, such as zebras, eat grass all day long. This is because grass has very little nutrition in it. Animals that eat meat, such as lions, get lots of nutrition from just one meal. Lions might only eat once a day, or once in several days.

Zebras

Monkey

What do monkeys eat?

Most monkeys eat plants, especially ripe fruit, berries, leaves, and shoots. They can climb trees in search of food, or they scrabble around on the forest floor looking for seeds, nuts, or insects to eat. Some monkeys also eat small animals, such as birds.

Why do rabbits need such big teeth?

Rabbits are plant eaters and they use their big teeth to slice up plants. They munch twigs, leaves, and bark—and this wears down their teeth. Unlike humans, rabbits' teeth keep on growing throughout their lives.

Think

Write down everything you ate yesterday. What did you eat? Did you eat meat, plants, or both?

Why do chimps use sticks?

Chimpanzees use sticks to help them get food. They poke sticks into termite nests and when they pull the sticks out, they are covered with yummy termites (that are just like ants). Chimps also bash nuts with stones and use sticks to fight one another.

Chimpanzee

Clever!

Chimps learn how to use tools such as sticks, by watching their mothers. Like many mammals, chimps are very clever animals.

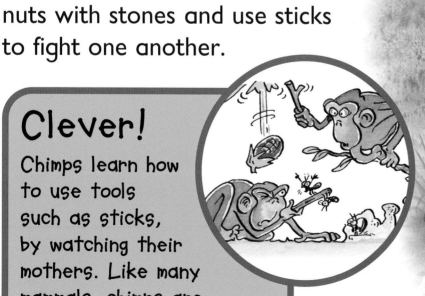

Why do sea otters carry stones?

Sea otters use stones to break open shelled sea creatures that they want to eat. Crabs, clams, and oysters are protected by hard shells. Sea otters know that the shells can be broken by a hard whack with a stone!

Sea otter

How can a mongoose break an egg?

The cusimanse is a mongoose that has a smart way of getting food out of shells. It throws an egg, or crab, between its hind legs and straight into a tree or stone—until it breaks!

Discover

Find out what tools you use every day. Think of how you eat, how you draw, and how you play.

Quiz time

Do you remember what you have read about mammals? These questions will test your memory. The pictures will help you. If you get stuck, read the pages again.

3. Which mammal is very bouncy?

page 9

4. Can seals breathe underwater?

page 10

1. What is a joey?

page 5

5. Are polar bears cuddly?

page 12

2. What is the biggest mammal?

page 6

6. Why are some animals white?

page 13

7. Why do wolves live in packs?

page 16

8. How many meerkats live together?

page 17

page 21

11. What do bears eat?

page 21

12. Why do dogs hunt in packs?

13. Are rhinos dangerous?

9. How big is a baby panda?

page 18

page 22

Answers

1. A baby kangaroo
2. The blue whale
3. The kangaroo
4. No
5. No, they are fierce hunters
6. To blend in with their surroundings
7. Because they hunt together and look after each other
8. Up to 30
9. As big as your hand
10. Calves
11. Insects, fruit and leaves
12. They are more likely to get something to eat
13. Yes, rhinos are one of the most dangerous animals

page 19

10. What are baby elephants called?

Index